THE
NEW TESTAMENT
UNFOLDED

Bible Readings delivered at the
Keswick Convention, 1954
by
W. GRAHAM SCROGGIE, D.D.

LONDON
PICKERING & INGLIS LTD.
1954

PICKERING & INGLIS LTD.

29 LUDGATE HILL, LONDON, E.C.4
229 BOTHWELL STREET, GLASGOW, C.2
Fleming H. Revell Company, 316 Third Avenue, Westwood, New Jersey
Home Evangel, 418 Church Street, Toronto

CONTENTS

I

THE FOUNDER AND FOUNDATIONS OF CHRISTIANITY
THE GOSPELS

II

THE GREATEST ADVENTURE OF ALL TIME
THE ACTS

III

A FAMOUS MISSIONARY'S CORRESPONDENCE
PAUL'S EPISTLES

IV

CHALLENGING VOICES AND THE GOAL OF HISTORY
THE GENERAL EPISTLES
AND THE
REVELATION

54497

I
THE FOUNDER AND FOUNDATIONS OF CHRISTIANITY

THE GOSPELS

IN a service I was conducting on one occasion, I announced that the Choir would sing 'Until the Day Break', and it was alleged that several people left the building!

I do not think you will leave when I announce my subject, because you are too far from home, but I trust that that will not be the reason why you do not go.

In these four mornings we are to consider, not a text, nor even a book of the Bible, but the whole of the New Testament.

I have chosen this large subject for various reasons: *first*, because of the admitted prevailing ignorance of the Bible; *secondly*, because of the large number of young people who are gathered for the Convention; *thirdly*, because I know how eager missionaries on furlough are for spiritual information and refreshing before they return to their work again; *fourthly*, because I covet for the younger ministers present a ministry that shall be at once informed and expository; and *fifthly*, because I trust we all shall realize that unless spiritual experience is firmly based upon the Scriptures —especially those of the New Testament—it is almost certain to be transient, and may easily prove disastrous. Experience must be rooted in knowledge if it is to last and to grow; and there is no short cut to Bible knowledge, as there is none to any other kind of knowledge.

Plans of reading based on a bit of the Old Testament, and a bit of the New Testament every day will leave one ignorant of the content and power of the Scriptures. We do not read any other books in that way. If as a result of our studies this week many of you will resolve that you will read the New Testament sensibly, expectantly, and believingly, you will quickly become conscious of pulsations of new life.

THE NEW TESTAMENT

The New Testament is a collection of 27 Writings, none very long and some very short, and although these Writings treat of many subjects they stand in an organic relation to one another, and constitute a sublime whole.

The *Gospels* and *Acts* are historical; the *Epistles* are doctrinal; and the *Revelation* is prophetical.

In the *Gospels* is the foundation of redemption; in the *Acts* and *Epistles* is its superstructure; and in the *Revelation* is its completion.

The *Gospels* tell of the past; the *Acts* and *Epistles* belong to the present; and the *Revelation* points to the future.

The subject of the *Gospels* is *The Christ;* of the *Acts* and *Epistles* it is *The Church;* and of the *Revelation* it is *The Consummation*.

From this it is evident that the New Testament Writings are organic and progressive, and no piecemeal reading of them can be a substitute for the study of them as a whole.

It is ambitious, if not presumptuous, to attempt to deal with these 27 Writings in the three hours alloted to me, but I must hazard the venture with humble hope.

The following is the plan:

To-day we are to consider the GOSPELS, which present *the Founder and Foundations of Christianity*.

In the second Reading we shall take the ACTS, which records *the Greatest Adventure of all Time*.

In the third Reading the subject will be the PAULINE EPISTLES, *a Famous Missionary's Correspondence*.

And in the fourth Reading we shall consider what remains of the New Testament, the GENERAL EPISTLES and the REVELATION, in which we hear *Challenging Voices*, and are shown the *Goal of History*.

As this year the *British and Foreign Bible Society* is celebrating its triple Jubilee it is well that special emphasis be put upon the Bible, the greatest Book in all the world, and of all time. He who is ignorant of the Scriptures of both Testaments is wanting in the highest culture. The day is past when the Bible can be treated with contempt, and they who criticise it without having read it, only advertise their colossal and condemnable ignorance.

The Bible has put our literature, our art, and our music hopelessly in its debt, and more than anything else it has given tone, colour, and substance to the language we speak day by day. It has also motivated and energised the greatest deeds that have ever been performed.

I would rather be intimate with the four pamphlets which are called the Gospels than with all the classics of Greece and Rome.

In an Essay on Dryden it is said of the English Bible that 'if everything else in our language should perish, it would alone suffice to show the whole extent of its beauty and power.'

Restrictions of time do not allow of any reference to the Old Testament, except to say that in it the New Testament is firmly rooted, and from it it emerges.

Four Gospels

AS we turn to the New Testament we are confronted with Four Pamphlets, which are called Gospels. They can all be read in about four hours, yet, though so brief, they are of greater value than any other writings, ancient or modern. They record the story of Jesus Christ, revealing His Person, and showing what, by His ministry, He has done for mankind.

These priceless Memoirs were not written by intellectuals or men of the Schools, but by four persons whom no Selection Committee would have looked at—a tax-gatherer, a batman to an Apostle, a medical doctor, and a fisherman mystic. These four men have written immortal literature, and they did so quite unconsciously.

Why Four Gospels?

But *why are there four records of Christ's Story?* Would not one have done? We must look for the answer to this question in Revelation and History.

THE ANSWER OF REVELATION

Revelation shows that the Redemption which was promised in pre-Christian times, and was accomplished by the atoning sacrifice of Christ, was not for the Jewish Race only, but for the whole world. 'God so loved the world that He gave His only begotten Son.'

The Redeemer, therefore, in His Person and Work was the complete answer to the deepest need of all mankind.

His manifestation had four aspects. *Officially* He was both a *Sovereign* and a *Servant;* and *Personally* He was both *Man* and *God.* It is of the utmost importance to see this, because it is the Person of the Redeemer that gives Redemption its effectiveness.

Now, prophecy anticipates these aspects of the Redeemer's Person. In Zech. ix. 9 it says, '*Behold thy King*'; in Isa. xlii. 1, '*Behold my Servant*'; in Zech, vi. 12, '*Behold the Man*'; and in Isa. xl. 9, '*Behold your God*'.

These are the four aspects of Christ's Person which are presented in the Four Gospels. He is the *Sovereign in Matthew;* the *Servant in Mark;* the *Man in Luke;* and *God in John.*

But a second group of prophecies anticipates these aspects of Christ's Person. In Jer. xxiii. 5 it says: 'I will raise *a righteous Branch—a King*'; in Zech. iii. 8, 'I will bring forth *my Servant, the Branch*'; in Zech. vi. 12, 'Behold *the Man whose name is the Branch*'; and in Isa. iv. 2, '*the Branch of the Lord shall be beauty and glory*'.

Here are four passages which predict Christ as *The Branch,* and in the four aspects of Sovereign, Servant, Man, and God, which again point to the Four Gospels respectively—*in Matthew the Sovereign; in Mark the Servant; in Luke the Man; and in John, God.*

Thus Revelation shows why there are Four Gospels, neither fewer, nor more.

THE ANSWER OF HISTORY

But in addition to Revelation, History shows why there are Four.

At the time of Messiah's Advent three great Races represented mankind—the *Jews,* the *Romans,* and the *Greeks,* and each of these had prepared for His coming.

Christ came to meet the deepest need of these Races and of all whom they represented, and how He did this the Gospels tell us.

From the second century it has been recognized that *Matthew's Gospel* was written for the *Jews;* that *Mark's* was written for the *Romans;* and that *Luke's* was written for the *Greeks;* and because from among all peoples a *Christian Church* was to emerge, a Fourth Gospel was made necessary which would be for all Christians. No one of these Gospels could present the whole truth about the Redeemer's work for mankind, but the Four together do so exhaustively.

These should be read continuously, with the distinctive character and purpose of each ever in view.

A. THE FOUNDER OF CHRISTIANITY

As we read these Records we shall see that one Age is ending, and another is beginning. *Judaism* of the Old Testament is passing, and *Christianity* of the New Testament is coming; and Christ is the fulfiller of the one, and the initiator of the other.

> 'When the fulness of the time came, God sent forth His Son'. (Gal. iv. 4.)
> 'God, having of old time spoken unto the fathers in the prophets by divers portions and in divers manners, hath at the end of these days spoken unto us in (His) Son'. (Heb. i. 1, 2).

He who was at once *Sovereign* and *Servant,* and *Man* and *God,* was the Founder of Christianity, and so the closest attention must be given to His Person as revealed in the Gospels.

The study of this subject is not the preserve of

theologians, but is the priceless privilege of all Christians. What, then, do the Gospels tell us about

THE PERSON OF CHRIST

Two facts are stated with the utmost emphasis: first, that Christ was *Human*; and secondly, that He was *Divine*.

His Humanity relates Him to the human race, and His Divinity relates Him to the Eternal God; and so He is the *God-Man*, bringing God to men, and leading men to God.

These facts constitute the mystery of His Person, and the truth of them is not affected by our inability to understand how these two natures could be united in one Person.

Let us look, then, first of all at

I. THE HUMANITY OF CHRIST

Everywhere in the Gospels this is assumed and declared, and the first thing we must note is that

1. CHRIST'S HUMANITY WAS REAL AND NOT FEIGNED

This is made evident in many ways, among which may be mentioned:

(i) *The Physical Life of Christ*

He was born into the world; He was a helpless babe, dependent on His mother; He was subject to the authority of a home; He grew in stature; He hungered and ate; He thirsted and drank; He worked and wearied; He felt the need of rest and slept; He learned a trade and worked at it for eighteen years; His body suffered pain and privation; He made many references to His body and its parts; and at last He died. These things can be true only of a human being.

(ii) *The Moral Life of Christ*

As a man Christ had an unswerving sense of duty, a penetrating consciousness of right and wrong which led Him to feel the pressure of temptation, and to resist it.

He recognized and accepted opportunity and responsibility. He was loyal to the social and political conditions of His time which it was no part of His mission directly to antagonize—as, for example, the practice of slavery, and Rome's rule of the Jews in Palestine.

Some of the moral ingredients in the character of Jesus were His love of God and man, self-control, self-denial, transparent sincerity, courage, calmness, patience, prudence, humility, endurance and goodness.

(iii) *The Emotional Life of Christ*

As man Christ entered fully into experiences of joy and sorrow. He exhibited wonder and surprise. He was no stranger to love and anger, nor to indignation and compassion.

He sought sympathy, and felt the pain of disappointment. More than once He wept. His gratitude and zeal were unmistakable; nor must we overlook His sense of humour.

(iv) *The Intellectual Life of Christ*

The foregoing characteristics could not be predicated of God, nor can what we speak of as Christ's intellectual life. It is written that He grew in wisdom, and what He knew as a man He must have learned.

He went to school, as did every Jewish boy, and His mind developed as our minds do, though, of course, much more rapidly.

At no time did He know everything. As man He was not omniscient, for omniscience is not a human attribute. He asked questions to elicit information, and acted on information which He received.

Proof of this is in the following passages:

> 'When Jesus heard of (the death of John the Baptist) He departed by ship into a desert place apart'. (Matt. xiv. 13).
>
> 'When Jesus heard (that Lazarus was dead) He abode two days still in the place where He was'. (John xi. 6.)
>
> When Jesus came to Bethany 'He found that (Lazarus) had lain in the grave four days already'; and He asked Mary where the grave was. (John xi. 17. 34.)
>
> Before feeding the multitude He asked His disciples, 'How many loaves have ye?' (Matt. xv. 34.); and on another occasion He asked: 'Who touched my clothes?' (Mark v. 30.)
>
> He asked the name of the demented Gadarene. (Mark v. 9.)
>
> He asked a father how long his son had been subject to fits. (Mark ix. 21.)
>
> He went to a fig tree to see if any figs were on it. (Mark xi. 13.)
>
> He plainly stated that He did not know the hour of a certain future event. (Mark xiii. 32.)

Christ's sense of wonder and surprise indicated that His mental life was conditioned; but it must be affirmed that His mind was not subject to error for it was unclouded by sin.

The existence of all-knowledge and limited knowledge in one and the same person is part of the mystery of the Incarnation, of the Divine and the human in one personality. No theory that we can frame can do justice to all the facts.

Without His perfect knowledge of Divine things Christ could not have been to us the manifestation of God; and without the mental experience involved in those conditions of acquiring knowledge we should not have had among us One who was 'in all points tried as we are'; there would have been something wanting in the perfection of His humanity.

It is for us to see and keep clear and distinct in our minds each fact of Christ's personality.

Unless one's judgment is sadly warped he cannot read what Jesus said, as recorded in the Gospels, without being deeply impressed by its simplicity and profoundness; its range and qualities.

His thinking was intuitive rather than discursive; concrete rather than abstract; positive rather than negative; and creative rather than critical.

No utterances of man have ever been as bracing as those of Jesus, for they are dateless, infallible, and authoritative.

Another evidence of the reality of His human nature was

(v) *The Social Life of Christ*

The Gospels show that Jesus lived a natural social life. He was a member of a family, having a mother, brothers and sisters. He attended a wedding feast, and accepted invitations to dinner. He had special friends, such as Martha, Mary, and Lazarus. He needed and wanted companionship, and He found it in the company of His apostles, and of those women who ministered to His temporal needs.

Attention must be called briefly to one more matter, viz.,

(vi) *The Religious Life of Christ*

This is a profound and difficult subject, but the essence of it consists in His relation as man to God.

Jesus revealed a deep sense of His dependence on God His Father, and apart from God He had no thoughts, desires, or will. This sense of dependence was repeatedly expressed: e.g., "The Son can do nothing of Himself"; and, 'The Father abiding in me doeth the works'.

An outstanding evidence and expression of Jesus' religious life was His habit of prayer, which is prominently recorded in the Gospels of Luke and John. God the Father never prays because He has no one to pray to, but Christ's life was a life of prayer; He had much to say on the subject of prayer; and some of His prayers are on record, notably in John xvii.

Another evidence of His religious life was His absorbing love for His Father, a love which was the atmosphere in which all His actions were performed, and all His feelings were determined.

The Gospel Records, then, make it abundantly clear that Christ's humanity was real and not feigned.

But a second fact must be considered which is of equal importance, namely that

2. CHRIST'S HUMANITY WAS PERFECT AND NOT FAULTY

The first fact is true of all men—that **our** humanity

2

is real and not feigned; but the second is true only of Christ.

The character portrayed in the Gospels could not have been created by any human mind, and so it must be a photo of facts.

In all the realm of biography the character of Christ stands apart and alone. Study the characters of Shakespeare, Scott, Dickens, Thackeray, George Eliot, and of all who have portrayed character, and it is easy to see in them the presence of qualities which should not be there, and the absence of qualities which should be there, but neither of these defects is found in the character of Jesus.

Look at a few of the facts which the Gospels disclose relative to the subject before us.

CHRIST HAD NO CONSCIOUSNESS OF SIN

Sensibilities which characterize the best of men were entirely wanting in Him. He never apologized for anything. He never said He was sorry for anything He had done. He never withdrew anything He had said, nor modified it. He never admitted having made a mistake. He never showed any sign of regret, or of remorse for misused or lost opportunities. He never exhibited any consciousness of guilt. He never acknowledged sin in Himself, and so never asked for pardon. He never felt the pain of an accusing conscience. He never showed any dread of the penal future. He never manifested any trace of healed scars, nor memories of defeat.

In all this the difference between Him and us is not one of degree, but of type. His was 'the one quite unspotted life that has been lived within our sinful race'. Had He not been sinless, to have made—as He did—such a claim for Himself, would of itself have been sin. It is perfectly clear that the piety of Jesus was impenitent and unrepentant.

CHRIST PERFECTLY COMBINED IN HIMSELF QUALITIES WHICH ARE COMMONLY REGARDED AS INCOMPATIBLES.

Of such we may mention.

Solemnity and Joyfulness (Mark x. 32. John xv. 11).

On the last journey to Jerusalem He was so solemn that His disciples were afraid; yet, in His last discourse, in the Upper Room, He repeatedly spoke of His joy.

Aloofness and Sociability (Mark i. 35. John ii. 1-10).

Rising up a great while before day He departed into a solitary place; yet, when He was called to a marriage feast He went.

Dignity and Humility (John xix. 9, 10. Matt. xi. 29).

Evidence of dignity is illustrated by His composed silence in the presence of Pilate; yet, of Himself He said: 'I am meek and lowly in heart'.

Profoundness and Simplicity

This is abundantly illustrated by the parables which Jesus spoke. These are so simple that any child will be attracted to them, and will understand them; yet they are so profound that they baffle every attempt to discover their final meaning. As long as language lasts these incomparable parables will draw and hold and thrill the serious mind.

Severity and Tenderness

He who lashed the Pharisees with His words (Matt. xxiii) said to the poor adulteress, 'Neither do

I condemn thee'. He who said to Peter, 'Get thee
behind me, Satan', said from the cross to the Apostle
John, 'Behold thy mother', committing to the Apostle
His own mother.

Energy and Restfulness

The unceasing activity of Jesus was astonishing.
From dawn to night He travelled and taught, and
performed works of mercy; and yet there is no evidence
that He was ever flustered or irritated, though, being
human, He did tire. His experience was one of
unbroken peace within; the peace which at last He
bequeathed to all His followers.

Haste and Leisureliness

One cannot read Christ's story without sensing a
certain urgency in His activities, especially towards
the close of His life, and yet throughout there was the
atmosphere of leisureliness. He was never so busy
as not to have time for those who needed Him.

The character of Jesus was held in perfect equilibrium.

He had no strong points because He had no weak ones.

Every one of us must be conscious of weaknesses and
defects, of insufficiencies and excesses, but Jesus had
no such consciousness because His character was
complete.

He who is so like us in some respects is profoundly
unlike us. He is alone and apart in a category of His own.

He was conscious that His relation to God was
unique, as when He said, 'I and My Father are one'.

He was conscious also of His distinction from men.
He never prayed with others; nor did He include
Himself in the prayer He taught His disciples.

He distinguished between His own and His disciples'
relation to God. He never said, 'Our Father', or
'Our God', but 'My Father, and your Father; my
God and your God'.

CHRIST'S HUMANITY AND OURSELVES

Now, belief in this Humanity of Christ is vital for
Christian faith. He who believes it believes that God
has come right down to us historically. He who
believes it believes in the possibility and actuality of
Atonement. And he who believes it believes that,
apart from sin, Christ is one of us, and one with us,
'touched with a feeling of our infirmity'; 'in all points
tempted like as we are', and so He is 'able to succour
them that are tempted'.

We must now turn to the second great truth revealed
in the Gospels, namely

II. THE DIVINITY OF CHRIST

There is no time to say anything about the Old
Testament anticipation of Christ's Divinity, nor of the
apostolic proclamation of it; but the Gospels declare
the fact in the most unmistakable way.

CHRIST'S CLAIMS FOR HIMSELF

Christ's claims for Himself are of the profoundest
importance, and it was because of these that the Jews
opposed Him, and eventually had Him crucified.

He claimed to transcend the Mosaic Law (Matt. v. 21,
22, 27. 28). He continuously preached Himself
(e.g., Matt. xi. 28-30). He promised that prayer
offered in His Name would be answered (John xiv. 13).

He declared His pre-existence (John viii. 58).

He claimed to be Lord of the realm of death
(John ii. 19). He invited men to trust in Him as they
trusted in God (John xiv. 1). He said that love of
Him was proof that one was a child of God (John viii.
42). He affirmed that no one knew God but Himself,
and those to whom He revealed Him (Matt. xi. 27).
He accepted the confession of Nathanael and of Peter
that He was the Son of God (John i. 49. Matt. xvi. 16).
He said that whoever had seen Him had seen the
Father (John xiv. 9, 10). He affirmed that He had
the power to forgive sins, and to give eternal life
(Matt. ix. 2. John x. 28). He claimed absolute
authority for His teaching (Matt. vii. 24, 26). He
declared that He had universal power (Matt. xxviii. 18).
He united Himself with the Father and the Spirit
as together constituting the Godhead (Matt. xxviii. 19);
and He asserted that God and He were One (John x. 30)

No one in history, unless blasphemously, has ever
made such claims, and if they be not true He Himself
was the greatest of all blasphemers.

Then, there are:

CHRIST'S CLAIMS UPON MEN

These are not less significant than His claims for
Himself, for they too point to His Divine nature and
authority. He claims the undivided devotion of men
and women, and declares that one's relation to Him
must take precedence over every other relation. The
great passage on this subject is Luke xiv. 25-33.

Christ also declares that only by coming to Him
can we be delivered from the burden of sin. He
affirms that only as we become like Him can we be

what we ought to be (Matt. xi. 28-30); and, most astonishing of all, perhaps, He says that only they who obey Him shall never die (John viii. 51).

The Divinity of Christ is not merely a theological conception or a matter only of academic interest, but a fact and truth of universal, age-long, and vital importance.

If Jesus was not God Christianity is a fraud, and the Christian Church is a farce. If Jesus was not God the Bible is a lie, and those who teach it are ignorant and deluded.

But 'the Word was with God, and the Word was God'.

Such, then, is the Founder of Christianity.

And now a word must be said, and all too briefly, about

B. The Foundations of Christianity

These relate to the whole Ministry of Christ the God-Man, and are resident in His teaching and work.

1. *THE TEACHING OF CHRIST*

This is a vast mine of riches, and invites the diligence of them who desire great spoil.

Matthew says, 'Jesus went about teaching', and we should want to know *how* and *what* He taught, that is, the manner and substance of His teaching.

(i) The Manner of Christ's Teaching

His teaching is absolutely *original*. Heathendom had had great teachers—Confucius, Buddha, Plato, Socrates, Aristotle, Caesar, Virgil and others; and Israel had had Moses, Isaiah, Jeremiah and others, but Christ owed nothing to any of them. 'Never man spake like this Man'

Another characteristic of His teaching is its *simplicity*. He always aimed at the greatest clearness in the briefest compass. His simplicity was not shallowness, as is seen in another characteristic—its *profoundness*. It was this that astonished all who heard Him and who said, 'Whence hath this man these things?' Another feature of His teaching is its *pregnancy*. Most speakers find it difficult to be compact without being obscure, but Christ taught in crisp pointed sentences which stick like burrs in the mind.

Other features of Christ's teaching, which there is not time to comment on, are its *concreteness*, its *picturesqueness*, its *appositeness*, its *practicability*, its *authoritativeness*, and its *finality*. These are subjects for the preacher for a year and more to come.

(ii) THE SUBSTANCE OF CHRIST'S TEACHING

But of more importance than the manner of Christ's teaching is its *substance*, that is, *what* He taught. He spent no time on trifles, but dealt with great subjects only—would that all preachers had done the same! His parables and other discourses are simply incomparable and exhaustless. I envy you younger men who have before you opportunities which lie behind me of preaching great things week by week. Leave philosophy, politics and economics alone, and preach Christ, the Kingdom, Salvation, Sin, Forgiveness, Love, Atonement, and scores of other commanding themes. This is what Christ did, and it is what He has called you to do.

The people are tired of ten minutes of platitudes

and inanities for sermons—give them the Bread of Heaven and the Wine of the Kingdom.

2. *THE WORK OF CHRIST*

Great as is the teaching of Christ the deepest Foundations of Christianity do not lie in it, but in His Work, and *His great Work was His Death*. He Himself declared this when He said, 'I came to give my life a ransom for many'.

The Gospels concentrate *historically* on this work, and the Epistles concentrate on it *doctrinally*. It was the theme of all the first preachers, as it has been of all the greatest preachers ever since; and it will be the substance of eternal song.

> 'Unto Him that loveth us, and loosed us from our sins by His blood . . . be the glory and the dominion for ever and ever': and the inhabitants of heaven will be those 'that washed their robes and made them white in the blood of the Lamb.' (Rev. i. 5, 6; vii. 14—R.V.)

Christ's interpretation of His death is the only true one, and the Gospels do not leave us in any doubt as to what that was. These Four Records draw us to the Cross, and from there to the empty tomb and the mountain top, and their last word is,

> 'Go ye into all the world, and preach the gospel to the whole creation'. (Mark xvi. 15.)

This is the revelation which the Gospels preserve, the revelation of Christ's Person and Work, which gave birth to Christianity, and is the secret of its continuance, and the guarantee of its final triumph.

The Four Gospels derive their value—not from the authors of them, nor from the time at which they were written—but from what they say, and if we would know who Christ was, and what He did, we must make these Records our constant companions, and must dwell in this wonderful realm of revelation. And

> 'Now unto Him who is able to do exceeding abundantly above all that we ask or think, according to the power that worketh in us, unto Him be the glory in the Church and in Christ Jesus unto all generations for ever and ever. Amen.' (Eph. iii. 20, 21.)

II

THE GREATEST ADVENTURE OF ALL TIME

THE ACTS OF THE APOSTLES

THE BOOK OF THE ACTS is one of the finest things in the literature of the world. In what is little more than a pamphlet the Story is told of how, out of what appeared to be tragic failure—the death of Christ— a Movement arose which was destined to conquer the world, and to establish a kingdom of truth and righteousness which shall never pass away.

The Story covers a period, not of a century or two, but of a single generation of 33 years—from A.D. 30 to A.D. 63—a period which is well within the life-time of most of us. This fact alone is astonishing because the progress of the greatest Movements is generally slow. Truly this is a Book of Words about Deeds!

We may estimate the value of a book by considering what the loss would have been if it had never been written. Judged in this way it is safe to say that if the 'Acts' had never been written there would have been a blank in our knowledge which nothing could have supplied.

Luke ends the Gospel which he wrote with the words—

> 'And it came to pass, while Jesus blessed His disciples, He was parted from them and carried up into heaven. And they worshipped Him, and returned to Jerusalem with great joy; and were continually in the Temple, praising and blessing God'. (Luke xxiv. 51-53.)

Omitting the 'Acts' there follow a number of Letters which would remain unintelligible to any reader. They would be as a maze without a clue; as a lock without a key. A hundred questions could be asked to which there would be no answers.

But supply the Book of the Acts and all is clear. It records that, for thirty-three years, Jesus continued 'to do and to teach' what He had commenced while He was on earth (i. 1). The 'Acts' is the first chapter of Church history, and the last chapter is not yet written. To be ignorant of this Book is something of which one should be thoroughly ashamed—not the Christian only, but everyone, because it is a vital part of human history.

PREPARATION FOR WORLD-EVANGELIZATION

How what is called *Christianity* spread from Jerusalem to Rome, from the Capital of Judaism to the Capital of the Empire, is the outstanding wonder of history; and for its accomplishment there had been—in the providence of God—*much preparation*.

This preparation is itself a historic wonder and a thrilling story, which we must look at, though all too briefly.

THE JEWISH DISPERSION

One of the factors in it was *the Dispersion of the Jews* (John vii. 35. James i. 1. 1 Peter i. 1).

Moses had predicted that if they apostatized they would be scattered, and this happened when they were taken into Assyrian and Babylonian captivity, and when later, and for other reasons, they spread Westward. This Dispersion helped to prepare the way for the spread of Christianity (Acts ii. 5, 9-11).

Synagogues

A second factor which helped this new Movement was *the institution of synagogues*. These were places where the Jews assembled for worship, and they existed wherever Jews were found; and so, when the evangelization of the world began, the Christian missionaries secured a footing wherever there were synagogues.

It was Paul's habit on visiting a place to go first of all to the Jews in their place of worship (Acts xiii. 14).

A Universal Language

A third factor in the spread of Christianity was *a universal language*. To-day missionaries going abroad are under the necessity of learning the language of the country to which they go, but in the apostolic age the Greek language was the common speech of all the nations which environed the Mediterranean, and it was spoken from Jerusalem to Rome. The advantage of this to the Christian missionaries is obvious.

The Septuagint

Related to this a fourth factor which assisted world-evangelization was *the Greek translation of the Old Testament Scriptures*, called the *Septuagint;* which, of course, could be read wherever Greek was spoken.

Roman Law and Roads

The spread of Christianity was aided also by a fifth factor, namely, the *Roman Law and Roman Roads*.

The Roman Law often protected the heralds of the Gospel, as the Book of the Acts shows (xviii. 12-16 xix. 35-41, *et al*); and *the Roman Roads*, which have outlasted the decay of 2000 years reached from the

Euphrates to Ephesus, and from the Adriatic to Rome, and along these the missionaries travelled unhindered with the Good News; and but for such roads the enterprise would have been well-nigh impossible.

DECAY OF PAGAN RELIGIONS

A sixth factor must be named, which helps to account for the rapid spread of Christianity in the first century of our era, namely, *the decay of the pagan religions*.

There was widespread disillusionment, spiritual hunger, and the quest for satisfaction. The world was crying after God, and its religions, even where they were still believed in, were unavailing (Acts xvii. 23).

It was into such a situation as this that the Gospel went with its message of pardon and peace, of new life and conquering power.

This, then, is the background of the New Testament.

THE CRUCIFIXION AND THE COMMISSION

Coming now to the circumstances immediately preceding the Story of the 'Acts', we can realize how hopeless the outlook appeared to be—the two things which strike us most are, *the Death of Christ*, and *the Commission of the Apostles*.

The leader of this little group of followers had been crucified, and all their hopes lay dead. Their state of mind is reflected in the words—'*We trusted that it was he who should redeem Israel*' (Luke xxiv. 21).

Verily the sun had gone out of their sky, but within half a week midnight darkness gave way to endless day. Jesus rose from the dead and appeared to His disciples; and at the end of forty days He said to them:

'All authority hath been given unto Me in heaven and in earth. Go ye, therefore, and make disciples of all the nations.'

'Go ye into all the world, and preach the gospel to the whole creation'.

'Ye shall be my witnesses . . . unto the uttermost part of the earth'.

(Matt. xxviii. 18, 19. Mark xvi. 15. Acts i. 8).

Such a commission seemed utterly absurd. Eleven unschooled men, about nine of whom we know little, were told to conquer the Roman Empire and the whole world. These were the men who, after the Crucifixion locked themselves in a room 'for fear of the Jews'. That they could do what was commanded seemed like a madman's dream.

But this is where *the Book of the Acts* comes in.

THE DESCENT OF THE HOLY SPIRIT

Ten days after the risen Lord had ascended to heaven an event occurred which has changed the whole course of history. While a hundred and twenty disciples, men and women. were gathered together for prayer in Jerusalem, the Holy Spirit descended upon them, and the Christian Church came into being, Christianity was born.

It was this coming of the Spirit upon the disciples which made possible the seemingly impossible—world-wide conquest.

The Lord had said:

'Ye shall receive power (the word is *dynamite*), *when the Holy Spirit is come upon you'* (Acts i. 8); and the dynamite of physics could be no match for the dynamite of Pentecost, though neither the world nor the Church seems to have learned this even yet!

In A.D. 30 began a Movement the aim and end of which was that *the kingdom of this world shall become the Kingdom of our Lord, and of His Christ, who shall reign for ever and ever* (Rev. xi. 15).

THE ASCENSION

When Christ ascended the disciples might well have felt orphaned, but He had said, '*It is expedient for you that I go away*'; and, '*I will not leave you orphans.*' (John xvi. 7; xiv. 18).

It was necessary that Christ should depart in order that His presence should be no longer local, but universal; and to compensate for His absence He gave to all believers the Holy Spirit, and thus a new age began.

It is the Book of the Acts which records historically the work of the Holy Spirit in and through the Christian Church.

PERIODS OF CHRISTIAN WITNESS

But the change-over from Judaism to Christianity, from what the Old Testament represents to what the New Testament represents, could not be made suddenly. There has never been a clean-cut division between Dispensations, but they have always overlapped, a fact to which the Book of the Acts presents most convincing evidence.

The Book falls into three distinct parts relative to Christian Witness. In chapters i-vii is the *Jewish Period* of it; in chapters viii-xii, the *Transition Period;* and in chapters xiii-xxviii, the *Gentile Period.*

These Periods clearly indicate the gradual but rapid progress of Christianity throughout the Roman Empire.

In the First, covering *seven years*, the Church was *Founded;* in the Second, lasting *ten years,* it was *Broadened;* and in the Third, representing *sixteen years,* it was *Extended.*

In the First Period the Church was composed of *converted Jews only;* in the Second Period, *Gentiles* also were admitted into the Christian Fellowship; and in the Third Period it was composed *chiefly of Gentiles.*

In A.D. 30 there were only a few hundred Christians, all Jews; and in A.D. 63, throughout and beyond the Roman Empire there must have been tens of thousands. If the same progress had been made since the apostolic age there would have been no paganism in the world to-day.

The Subject of Christian Witness

Before He ascended the Lord said to His Apostles:

> 'Ye shall receive power when the Holy Spirit is come upon you; and *ye shall be my witnesses* both in Jerusalem, and in all Judaea and Samaria, and unto the uttermost part of the earth'. (Acts i. 8).

That is the key to the Book of the Acts, and it defines the mission of the Christian Church until Christ returns.

We are not commissioned to *advocate* the Gospel, but to *proclaim* it, not to *argue* about the Good News, but to *announce* it, and what we are to bear witness to is—*that Christ died for our sins, and that he rose again from the dead, and that there is none other name under heaven given among men whereby we must be saved* (1 Cor. xv. 3, 4. Acts iv. 12).

This was the Message of the Apostolic Church, and

it has been the Message of every spiritual revival in the history of the Church since then. The periods of spiritual barrenness in Church history are all attributable to the denial or neglect of this Message.

The application of the Gospel is as varied as are circumstances, but the Message of the Gospel itself is unchanging.

The central *Subject* of Christian witness is *the Redeeming Christ;* the widening *Sphere* of it is from Jerusalem *to the ends of the earth;* the exclusive *Source* of it is *the Christian Church;* and the unfailing *Secret* of it is *the Holy Spirit!*

Let us now look at each of these periods of Witness which the Acts records.

I. THE JEWISH PERIOD OF THE CHURCH'S WITNESS

Acts i-vii

There is only time to indicate the salient features of this first seven years of Church history. These features can be summarized in seven words: *Founding, Testimony, Opposition, Discipline, Testing, Organization,* and *Persecution.*

THE CHURCH

1. *The Church was Founded on the Day of Pentecost* (Acts ii. 1-13).

By the Descent and Baptism of the Holy Spirit all believers then living were constituted a Church, a Body for Christ, through which, in His absence, He can function in the world.

The Christian Church is not the aggregate of the

many denominational Christian churches, but the aggregate of all regenerated persons—men, women, and children, and of these as indwelt by the Holy Spirit. The New Testament knows no other.

THE TESTIMONY

2. The Church thus founded was commissioned to bear a *Testimony* (Acts ii. 14-47), and, as to its character, this Testimony was—and was to continue to be—twofold. It was to consist in a *simple creed* (Acts ii. 14-41) and in *sanctified conduct* (Acts ii. 42-47).

True Christianity has never divorced these things. Belief and practice are related to one another as are *cause* and *effect*, *centre* and *circumference*, *foundation* and *superstructure;* and so, in Acts ii, following a report of Peter's Pentecostal Sermon is a description of the life of the first Church.

> 'Day by day, continuing steadfastly with one accord in the Temple, and breaking bread at home, they did take their food with gladness and singleness of heart, praising God, and having favour with all the people'. (46, 47.)

OPPOSITION

3. But wherever Christ works the devil becomes active, and so we see that the Church just described met with strong *Opposition* (Acts iii. 1-iv. 31). What the rulers, who had arrested Peter and John for healing a man, lacked in weight they made up for in numbers, and for sensible argument they substituted abuse. But contempt is always contemptible, except when we 'pour contempt on all our pride'.

If we are doing God's will and work, we should not be surprised if we are opposed, nor should we complain.

DISCIPLINE

4. What, however, is much more serious than the opposition of the world or of a spurious religion is trouble within the Church itself. The occasions of this at the beginning were Ananias and Sapphira who together acted a lie, and brought upon themselves righteous judgment (Acts iv. 32-v. 16). This was the first exercise of *discipline* in the apostolic Church, but not the last (1 Cor. v. 5. 1 Tim. i. 20). To-day Church discipline seems to be entirely unknown, and surely this largely accounts for the weakness and ineffectiveness of many churches. The strength of a Christian Church cannot be determined by the *number* of its members, but by their *quality* (Acts v. 12, 13).

TESTING

5. Now follows the first *Testing* of the Church, which arose when the Sanhedrin put the Apostles into prison because of their growing success (Acts v. 17-42); and although this involved suffering the Apostles were delivered, and '*ceased not to teach and to preach Jesus as the Christ*' (Acts v. 42).

What is untested is unsafe. The bridge is tested by weight, the student by examination, the soldier by battle, and the Christian by trials (cf. 1 Peter i. 6, 7). This is inevitable, and only what may be expected.

ORGANIZATION

6. We are now shown that as the Church grew and new situations arose a certain amount of *Organization* became necessary (Acts vi. 1-6); and this was first occasioned by complaints that certain widows did not get a fair share of the funds provided to help the poor

and needy. Out of this discontent there arose in the Church the first office by appointment—that of *Deacon*, in the New Testament sense of the word. Since then there has been much Church organization; some of it wise, and some of it otherwise!

PERSECUTION

7. It was out of this organization that there came the first great *Persecution* of the Church, and the first martyrdom (Acts vi. 7-viii. 3). After preaching an epoch-making sermon, *Stephen*, one of the deacons, was stoned to death, and was the first of 'the noble army of martyrs' who have refused to deny the Christian faith.

Verily this was a wonderful seven years! The Church was well and surely launched on her eventful voyage. Truths were proclaimed, principles were exhibited, and standards were established which were to outlive all opposition and error, and ultimately to triumph over all evil.

But the Gospel could not for long be confined to a privileged Race and a single City. The new wine was bound to burst the old wine-skins, and so, in this classic record we are next told of

II. THE TRANSITION PERIOD OF THE CHURCH'S WITNESS
Acts viii-xii

No one can pass from chapter vii to chapter xiii of this Book without realising that something is required to account for the great change that has taken place. In the First Period the dominating personality was

Peter, but in the Third Period it is Paul. In the First
Period the Church's activities were confined to Jerusalem, but in the Third Period they are reaching out
westward to all mankind. In the First Period the
composition of the Church was entirely Jewish, but
in the Third Period it is chiefly Gentile.

How this great change came about Period Two
explains.

In the next ten years (A.D. 37-47) events took place
which were to give an entirely new complexion to the
New Movement. What these events were, Period Two
of the Acts relates.

We read that Stephen's testimony and death pre-
cipitated a '*great persecution against the Church in Jerusalem;
and all the Christians, except the Apostles, were scattered
throughout the region of Judaea and Samaria*'; and '*those
who were scattered went about preaching the word*' (Acts
viii. 1, 4).

The devil did a good thing that day for Christianity!
He took the precious seed which was in the Jerusalem
granary and threw it to the winds, and these carried
it to new soil where it was to produce a rich harvest.

PHILIP'S PREPARATION

1. Philip the Evangelist went to Samaria and pro-
claimed Christ, and there were many converts. When
Peter and John heard of this they went down to the
City and confirmed the good work, and on the return
journey they '*preached the Gospel to many villages of the
Samaritans*'.

Meanwhile Philip gave the Gospel to an Ethiopian
Court Official, and in this way introduced the Good
News to Africa (Acts viii. 4-40).

This was the beginning of the preparation for the wider witness.

SAUL'S PREPARATION

2. The next event was one of the most momentous in history—*the conversion of Saul of Tarsus* (Acts ix).

The greatest persecutor of the early Christians was suddenly and miraculously brought into contact with the Risen Christ, and instantly became a Christian.

This man, as we shall see, became the father of Foreign Missions, the founder of Churches right across Asia Minor and in eastern Europe, and the theologian of the Christian Church.

The late Earl of Birkenhead in his book '*Turning Points in History*' says that Paul '*altered the whole face of the world*'.

By the conversion of this man the preparation for the wider witness was immensely advanced.

PETER'S PREPARATION

3. The next recorded event was scarcely less momentous—*the visit of Peter to Cornelius at Caesarea* (Acts x).

This was nothing less than the formal recognition that all Gentiles, on equal terms with all Jews, had a right to the blessings of the Gospel, and to membership in the Christian Church.

This revelation, which had been anticipated in the Old Testament, Peter received in a vision vouchsafed to him at Joppa, in which he was told by a Voice from heaven that the Gentiles were no longer to be regarded as common and unclean; and when, later, he addressed Cornelius and the Gentiles gathered in his house, he said: '*Truly I perceive that God shows no partiality, but in every nation any one who fears Him and does what is right is acceptable to Him*'. (Acts x. 34).

By this event another great stride forward had been taken in preparation for the wider witness.

THE APOSTLES' PREPARATION

4. The fourth step was taken when, after Peter had related to *the Apostles* at Jerusalem what had happened, they recognized the tremendous significance of the event, and said: '*Then to the Gentiles also God has granted repentance unto life*' (Acts xi. 18).

THE CHURCH'S PREPARATION

5. A fifth and final step was taken in preparation for the wider witness when *the whole Church accepted the new situation.*

A new centre of operations was founded at *Antioch in Syria,* where the Gentiles on a considerable scale had the Gospel preached to them, and in the Church there the great missionary movement commenced, the record of which constitutes the third division of the Book of the Acts.

The preparation of *Philip,* and *Saul,* and *Peter,* and the *Apostles,* and the *Jerusalem Church* for world-wide evangelization—and all within ten years—indicates what the Holy Spirit can and will do when He is given the opportunity. And now opens—

III. THE GENTILE PERIOD OF THE CHURCH'S WITNESS
Acts xiii-xxviii

The magnitude and marvel of this Period make it

difficult to outline it within our appointed time, and all we can here attempt is to call attention to certain outstanding facts.

PAUL

1. There is, first of all, *the fact of Paul*, who was one of the greatest men God ever made. His intellectual power, his splendid courage, his determined perseverance, his understanding sympathy, his perfect integrity, his consummate tact, and his lateral humour show him to be a man of rich personality; and for the accomplishment of the task to which he was called these qualities were essential.

We can readily understand that neither Peter nor John could have succeeded in this enterprise of world-evangelization.

In another respect also was Paul providentially equipped for his great task. He was born *a Hebrew of Hebrews*, he was trained in *a Greek environment*, and he possessed *Roman citizenship*, and these privileges made his approach and appeal universal. No other Christian of the first century who is known to us had the advantages of *Semitic fervour, Greek versatility,* and *Roman standing* which characterized Paul, but God equips and endows His servants for what He wants them to do.

TRAVEL

2. Another fact which makes this missionary enterprise one of the wonders of history relates to *travel*.

In those days facilities for communication, which are commonplaces to us, did not exist. There were *no railways, no motor cars, no aeroplanes, no passenger ships*

—except such as were specially hired to take Jews to the Passover, and *no hotels*, as we understand that institution. The land journeys mentioned in the New Testament were made for the most part on foot, because most travellers could not afford horses or carriages, and the rate of progress was not more than 17 to 20 Roman miles a day.

With these facts in mind, think for a moment of Paul's journeys.

It is not an exaggeration to say that from the beginning of the first missionary venture to the time of Paul's death he travelled *on foot 5,580 miles*, and *by sea, 6,770 miles, a total of 12,350 miles*. Add to this that he was a *sick man* (2 Cor. xii), and that his sea journeys were made in cargo vessels, and we shall begin to realise the magnitude and the magnificence of what he did.

Four Journeys

3. In the light of all this it is deeply impressive that Paul made *four missionary journeys*, which took him from Antioch to Spain, and on each of these he founded Churches, and appointed elders, giving special attention to such strategic places as *Ephesus, Philippi*, and *Corinth*.

His pastoral concern for his converts was exhibited in repeated visits to many of his Churches, and by his much correspondence by agents and letters.

Flogging, stoning, shipwreck, hunger, thirst, cold, exposure, and sleepless nights did not destroy this man's love for the Lord, nor his determination to proclaim the Gospel throughout the Roman Empire (2 Cor. xi. 23-28).

And, let us remember, if we exclude Paul's imprisonments, all his missionary work was accomplished in about ten years (A.D. 47-58).

Having regard for the conditions which he confronted and the sufferings which he endured, our Christian service looks like play. To read Paul's story in the Acts should both humble and inspire us.

THE HOLY SPIRIT

4. But the outstanding Fact and Factor in the great missionary enterprise recorded in the Acts was *the Holy Spirit*. He is named 58 times in these 28 chapters, but He dominates the entire narrative. At every turn and in every crisis He is present in one or other of His many capacities.

He is the *Spirit of Promise* at the time of the Ascension (i); the *Spirit of Power* at Pentecost (ii); the *Spirit of Healing* to the lame man (iii); the *Spirit of Boldness* in Peter and John (iv); the *Spirit of Judgment* to Ananias and Sapphira (v); the *Spirit of Administration* in the appointment of Deacons (vi); the *Spirit of Steadfastness* in the martyr Stephen (vii); the *Spirit of Evangelism* in Peter and Philip (viii); the *Spirit of Quickening* to Saul of Tarsus (ix); the *Spirit of Guidance* to Peter and Cornelius (x); the *Spirit of Wisdom* in Barnabas (xi); the *Spirit of Deliverance* to imprisoned Peter (xii); the *Spirit of Missions* from Antioch to Rome (xiii-xxviii); the *Spirit of Councils* at the great Jerusalem Conference (xv); the *Spirit of Praise* in the imprisoned Paul and Silas at Philippi (xvi); *the Spirit of Opportunity* to Paul at Athens (xvii); the *Spirit of Watchfulness* in the Elders of the Church (xx); and the *Spirit of Courage* in Paul during his many captivities (xxi-xxviii).

One wonders at times whether the visible Churches are rejecting or silencing the Holy Spirit; whether ministers are depending more on their ability and industry than on Him who is the Power of all spiritual success; and whether the registered members of the Churches are relying more on organization and sundry other influences than on Him who was sent by God to sanctify and energize His people.

The Book of the Acts is still the revelation and standard of what Christ expects of His Church. The great notes of the Story are: *proclamation of the Gospel; personal testimony; persistent prayer; courageous faith; radiant joy; world-wide vision; dedicated personality,* and *utter reliance on the Holy Spirit.*

What a Book is this! The stage of the record is crowded with people, men and women, young and old, good and bad. Some, like Peter and Paul, shine like suns in the midnight sky, and others, like stars scarcely visible, have their place in the glory of the firmament. Apostles, Evangelists, and Deacons are here; Jews and Gentiles; and Rulers like Herod, Felix, Festus, and Gallio. Here flourishing Churches arise on pagan soil, as at Antioch, Ephesus, Philippi, and Corinth. It is here that we read of the first apostolic miracle; the first apostolic sermon; the first persecution of Christians; the first Church Synod; the first Gentile convert; the first Church organization; the beginnings of Christian Missions; and the origins of Christianity and the universal Church.

One apostle commits suicide, and another is murdered. One Christian woman lies and dies, another gives her only son to the cause of world-evangelization, and another entertains in her home a group of travelling missionaries. Peter raises a dead girl, and Paul, a dead boy. When the preachers are flogged they sing. A Roman centurion is converted to Christianity, and an Idumaean King is consumed by worms. Angels open prison doors, and a missionary takes charge of a troop ship.

The Book of the Acts has great values, historical, literary, dispensational, doctrinal, biographical, missionary, and spiritual. It was written by a Greek doctor of medicine who tells what, in thirty-three years, the Holy Spirit did in and through men and women who yielded themselves to Christ. These people were not faultless, and were not always blameless, but God chose, and still chooses, the world's foolish to confound the wise, the weak to put to shame the strong, and the nobodies to bring to nought all worldly somebodies.

The greatest military achievements dwindle when compared with the conquests of the unarmed soldiers of the Cross.

It is little wonder that the record of this greatest adventure of all time should end on the words— 'openly and unhindered'.

This adventure and achievement are not something to be admired only, but to be repeated to-day by the selfless courage of Spirit-filled men and women.

World-wide quickening and revival are more urgently needed to-day than ever they have been, but these blessings will not come by our unbelieving hesitations, our sectarian rivalries, our ignorant criticisms, our worldly indulgences, our unspiritual prejudices, our pathetic officiousness, and our rootless faith.

Apostolic success will come only by apostolic courage, and venture, and selflessness, and, be it remembered, it is the message and not the method that matters.

> *'Oh, Lord, send the power just now,*
> *and baptize every one'.*

III

A FAMOUS MISSIONARY'S CORRESPONDENCE

PAUL'S EPISTLES

LETTER WRITING

THE art of writing is of remote antiquity, and of all forms of it letter-writing is the most intimate and personal. A title with which we are familiar is 'The Life and Letters of . . .' e.g., Samuel Rutherford, or Robert Murray McCheyne. This title relates Letters to Life, and not without good reason, for the letters of anyone are a revelation of himself as no other form of writing can be. Before John Morley wrote the famous biography of Mr. Gladstone he examined over 50,000 of the Statesman's letters.

William Cowper's letters have been pronounced 'the most charming ever written in the English language', and the reason given for this verdict is that he just talked on paper, with no idea of publication.

LETTERS IN THE BIBLE

There are over fifty references to letters in the Bible, and not a few examples of such are in both the Old and the New Testament.

The first Christian letter was issued by a Council in Jerusalem about the year A.D. 50, and in it occurs the statement: 'It seemed good to the Holy Spirit and to us' (Acts xv. 28), which shows that what was written was Divinely as well as humanly directed; and this applies to all Paul's Epistles.

Paul's Correspondence

In the first century there was *no postal system* as we know it, and travelling was slow, and so, in consequence, correspondence was almost entirely confined to Imperial and official needs.

It should be remembered also that correspondence was written on *perishable materials*, with the result that much of it has been lost. This is true, not only of Imperial correspondence, but also of apostolic. It is probable that most of Paul's letters have perished, for it cannot be supposed that he wrote only thirteen. Indeed he tells us of other letters which have not survived. In 2 Thess. iii. 17—one of his earliest Epistles —he says: 'The salutation of me Paul with mine own hand, *which is the token in every epistle*'. This indicates that the Church at Thessalonica was not the first to which he wrote. Also, in 1 Cor. v. 9 he says: '*I wrote unto you in an epistle*', which shows that First Corinthians was not the first to that Church.

What concerns us, however, is not the Epistles which have been lost, but those which in the providence of God have been preserved.

Let us feel the full impact of the fact that of the twenty-seven Writings which constitute the New Testament twenty-one of them are epistles. It will be well for us to think of them sometimes as letters, for one small boy thought that an epistle was the wife of an apostle!

Contact by Letters

New circumstances create new requirements, and when Paul set out on his missionary journeys, made converts, and established Churches in Asia Minor, Macedonia and Greece, there arose the need for maintaining contact with the growing Christian community, and this could be done only by visitation and correspondence; and as Paul could not frequently revisit the Churches he established, communication by letter became a necessity.

Churches and converts needed comfort and encouragement; personal, social, doctrinal, and religious problems demanded apostolic attention; evils which threatened or existed had to be dealt with; abuses had to be reproved and corrected, and other matters were continually arising which made correspondence necessary and urgent.

Religious treatises or essays, disquisitions and compendiums of theology could not meet these multiform needs; what was required was the spontaneous and unstudied contact which letters alone could provide, and so there arose a new category of literature—*the Apostolic Letter*.

NEED AND SUPPLY

Schism, immorality, marriage problems, heathen food, difficulties related to public worship, speaking with tongues, and doctrinal error in Corinth necessitated the writing of a Letter to the Church there.

The relation to one another of the Law and the Gospel, which was a problem to the Galatian converts, led Paul to write an Epistle to the group of Churches in that Province. Misunderstanding about the Second Advent of the Lord was responsible for the Thessalonian Letters. Heresy concerning the Person and Work of Christ drew from the Apostle the Colossian Letter.

4

The conversion of a runaway slave led Paul to write his incomparable Note to Philemon. Gratitude is expressed in a letter to the Philippians for some money they had sent to the Apostle.

From this, and the occasions of the other Letters which Paul wrote, we see that his correspondence was something entirely new, and quite distinct from the Classic Writings of Cicero, Seneca and Pliny. Only by reading the Epistles in their setting can we expect to understand them. Paul's Letters are non-literary products, and were written in the common language of the people.

PAUL'S LETTERS ARE IN GROUPS

Before considering the fundamental message of these Letters we should know that they fall into four distinct groups which are separated from one another by about four years.

The first group—*1-2 Thessalonians*—is about *Christ's Second Coming*. The second group—*1-2 Corinthians, Galatians, and Romans*—relates to *the conflict of Christianity with Heathenism*. The third group—*Ephesians, Colossians, Philemon and Philippians*—is chiefly about *the Person of Christ and the life of the Christian in Him*. The fourth group—*1 Timothy, Titus, and 2 Timothy*—is what may be called the *Minister's Manual*, and deals with *personal conduct* and *Church organization*.

Seven of these thirteen Epistles were written to Churches at Rome, Corinth, Philippi, Colossae, and Thessalonica; two of them were written to groups of Churches, the Galatian and Ephesian Epistles; and four of them were written to individuals, the Epistles to Philemon, Titus, and Timothy.

These priceless Letters, written within a period of fifteen years, show how the divinest views of life penetrate into its meanest emergencies. We cannot read them too often, or know them too well. They are both theological and experimental, and are Writings absolutely unique in the religious history of the world.

THE FUNDAMENTAL MESSAGE OF THE LETTERS

And now it must be said that though these Letters were written at different times, to different people, and about different matters, there is discernible in them an underlying unity, a fundamental message, which transcends the local and transient circumstances which first occasioned them.

Beyond what the Apostle could know, the Holy Spirit was inspiring these Letters for the edification and sanctification of the universal Church of God till Christ returns.

The local circumstances of the apostolic Churches gave rise to matters of vital importance to all Christians throughout the Christian age, and so these Letters are of more significance to-day than they could possibly have been eighteen hundred years ago. As much as ever it is true that 'the Word of God is living and active'.

A boy who had received on his birthday some sweets, a watch, and a Bible, was asked what he had done with his presents, and he said: 'the sweets are gone, the watch is going, but the Word of the Lord endureth for ever.' How right he was!

'IN CHRIST'

What then is the underlying and fundamental message of Paul's Letters? It is found, it may be said, in two words, '*in Christ*', a preposition and a name which, in conjunction, give the key not only to Paul's Epistles but to the whole New Testament.

In the catacombs, the subterranean cemeteries of over seven millions of Christians, including a host of martyrs, there were many symbols and inscriptions the meaning of which was known only to believers. Among these were the *dove*, the *ark*, the *anchor*, the *palm*, the *fish*, the *hart*, the *olive*, the *harp*, the *cock*, and the *phoenix;* and in one of the many inscriptions were the words ἐν χριστω, 'In Christ'. These symbols and inscriptions show that to the early Christians their religion was one of joy and not of gloom, of life and not of death. Not for them were broken columns, fallen rosebuds, inverted torches, crucifixes, cypresses, and skeletons. Theirs were symbols of beauty, hope, and peace.

For the early suffering Christians the words 'in Christ' had a tremendous meaning, a meaning which enabled them to bear their witness to their Lord, and to endure their tortures even to death, with both courage and gladness. Outstanding examples of this are the two old men *Ignatius* and *Polycarp;* and the three young women, *Blandina*, *Felicitas*, and *Perpetua*.

ENSPHERED

The words '*in Christ*' or their equivalents occur about 130 times in the Epistles, which shows how important they are. They declare that Christ is the *sphere* of the Christian's life. The believer is not *encircled* in Christ, but *ensphered*. The difference is that a *circle* surrounds us on one plane only, but a *sphere* envelopes us in every direction and on every plane.

As the fish is ensphered in the sea, and the bird, in the air, so 'in Christ' the believer 'lives and moves and has his being'.

Now, this enspherement 'in Christ' implies several great truths. It means that we are *surrounded*— Christ is on every side of us; that we are *separated*— spiritually we are not in the realm of the world at all; that we are *safeguarded*—we can be attacked by enemies only through Christ; and that we are *supplied*; all we now and ever can need is 'in Christ' for us.

These blessings do not attach to the idea of encirclement, but 'in Christ' they are ours, whether or not we believe it and enjoy it.

We have an illustration of the *safeguarding* in the fact that Satan had to get God's permission before he could attack Job, and he still has to get such permission.

An examination of Paul's Epistles will reveal that in each of them some definite aspect is presented of our blessings 'in Christ'. Let us look at this.

In Romans We are Justified 'In Christ'

Paul writes: '*Justified* freely by His grace through the redemption that is "in Christ Jesus"' (iii. 24).

The word *Justification* and its cognates occur in this Epistle over sixty times. The first half of the Epistle is saturated with the idea, and, more than any other Epistle, it reveals the meaning of this blessing.

Justification has a fivefold cause. *The originating cause is God's grace* (iii. 24). *The efficient cause is Christ's blood* (v. 9). *The instrumental cause is our faith* (v. 1) *The assuring cause is Christ's resurrection* (iv. 25), and *the evidential cause is good works,* which the latter half of Romans (xii-xv.) proves and illustrates.

The blessing of justification includes many others. It involves and assures *forgiveness of sins, reconciliation to God, present peace,* and *salvation from the divine wrath because of sin;* and all these blessings we have '*in Christ Jesus*', so that they are absolutely secure.

IN 1 CORINTHIANS WE ARE SANCTIFIED 'IN CHRIST'

The Church at Corinth was the least spiritual of all the Pauline Churches. It was rent by schism; it harboured immorality; some members of it got drunk at the Lord's Table; the public worship was carried on in a disorderly fashion; and the resurrection was being denied by some.

Yet, writing to this Church Paul begins by saying that they '*are sanctified in Christ Jesus, called saints*' (i. 2).

This fact illuminates the doctrine of sanctification. It shows that it refers primarily, not to spiritual attainment, but to *relationship to God*. In this sense all Christians are 'saints', however unsaintly they may be. The justified person is separated unto God 'through the offering of the body of Christ' (Heb. x. 10). The Christian is 'set apart' unto God as of old animals and property were set apart.

But this is not the whole truth. The New Testament teaches that there should be an internal change in the believer corresponding to his relation to God. He who *is* holy should *become* holy. What is once for all *complete* by the work of the Son, is to be *progressively realized* by the action of the Spirit, with the co-operation of the believer (2 Cor. vii. 1).

By *regeneration* a new principle of life is implanted in the soul, and by *sanctification* all the faculties of the soul are more and more brought into conformity to this spiritual principle; and all this is done '*in Christ*'.

Christ is the sphere and the Spirit is the atmosphere of the sanctified life.

In 2 Corinthians We Are Vindicated 'In Christ'

Paul had been viciously attacked and bitterly slandered in the Church at Corinth, and in four chapters (x-xiii) in his second Epistle to them he answers his calumniators as one who is really beyond their reach, eternally 'ensphered *"in Christ"*.' He says: 'Think ye all this time that we are excusing ourselves unto you? In the sight of God speak we '*in Christ*' (xii. 19).

From these caustic chapters we see that there are times when it is right to answer attacks made upon us, but we must be very sure that the answer is made '*in Christ*'. No doubt, for the most part, it is better not to answer, but to leave our vindication to God and to history.

In Galatians We Are Liberated 'In Christ'

There are eleven references in this Epistle to freedom or liberty, and this freedom, it is affirmed, is '*in Christ*'. Paul speaks of certain persons who came 'to spy out our liberty which we have *in Christ Jesus*' (ii. 4); and throughout the Epistle he contrasts bondage and freedom, the one imposed by the Law, and the other imparted by the Gospel.

Many of the Galatian Christians were in danger of reverting to the bondage of Judaism, and against this Paul warns them. The believer is a 'bondslave' '*in Christ*', but he is not in 'bondage'. Our freedom is His grand control.

Galatians is the Epistle of Christian liberty, the charter of our emancipation, the battle-axe of Luther, and the watch-word of the true. '*In Christ*' we are free from the Law, free from self, and free from the world (ii. 19, 20; v. 24; vi. 14), and we are exhorted to 'stand fast in the *liberty* wherewith Christ has made us *free*, and not be *entangled* again with the yoke of *bondage*.'

In Ephesians We Are Exalted 'In Christ'

In this Epistle of only six chapters the expressions '*in Christ*', '*in Christ Jesus*', '*in the Lord*', '*in Him*', and their equivalents occur thirty-two times, and the privileges thus spoken of are due to the truth and fact that, not only did we die in Christ's death, and were raised in His resurrection, but also we are 'seated in the heavenlies in Him' (ii. 6).

How little we apprehend and appreciate the truths about ourselves which this Epistle reveals. '*In Christ*' we are chosen, adopted, accepted, redeemed, forgiven, resurrected, sealed, unified, and exalted. These are facts which are not affected by our feelings; they are truths to be trusted and tested, and because these blessings are all ours '*in Christ*' nought can rob us of them.

In Philippians We Are Exultant 'In Christ'

Philippians is the Epistle of Christian joy, an idea which occurs sixteen times in its four chapters. The explanation of it is in Paul's statement—'*I rejoice in the Lord*' (iv. 10). Christ is the source, substance, and sphere of the Christian's joy. This quality differs from *happiness*, which depends on what *happens*, for it is not determined or affected by circumstances. We cannot always be happy, but we should always rejoice.

When Paul wrote this radiant Epistle he was in
prison; and we must not forget that it was in the
shadow of Calvary that Jesus prayed that His followers
might share His joy (John xvii. 13; xvi. 22, 24).

Is it not true that this quality of joy has largely
dropped out of the Christian's experience! It is a
'fruit of the Spirit' (Gal. v. 22), and will become our
normal experience only when we realize that Christ
is the sphere of our life.

IN COLOSSIANS WE ARE COMPLETE 'IN CHRIST'

Ephesians and Colossians are twin Epistles. In the
former it is shown that the Church is Christ's Body,
and in the latter, that Christ is the Church's Head;
and it is here that Paul makes the profound statement:

> 'In Him dwelleth all the fulness of the Godhead
> bodily, and *ye are complete in Him*'. (ii. 9, 10).

Fulness is a key word and thought in this Epistle,
occurring at least eight times; and it is revealed that all
of God is in Christ, and all in Christ is for us, so that
as there is nothing lacking in Him there can be nothing
lacking to us. We are already 'complete in Him',
and are progressively to become complete by the
operations of the Holy Spirit in us.

The Colossian Epistle is addressed 'to the holy and
faithful brethren *in Christ, in Colossae*' (i. 2). What a
world of meaning is in this description—'*in Christ,
in Colossae*'! These believers lived in two localities,
one earthly, and the other heavenly. They dwelt in a
small town, and also they dwelt in the Eternal Lord.
When the Apostle John was 'in the isle' of Patmos,
he was also 'in the Spirit'. Every Christian lives in

two environments, the local and temporary, and the divine and eternal; and which of these dominates our consciousness is what matters.

IN 1 THESSALONIANS WE ARE EXPECTANT 'IN CHRIST'

Everywhere in this Epistle we see the shining of Christ's Advent feet, and this promised event is the *hope* of the Christian and of the Church. Paul begins the Letter by speaking of the *'patience of hope in our Lord Jesus Christ'* which characterized the Thessalonian believers (i. 3).

Hope in the New Testament never means *wistful longing*, but *glad certainty*. That Christ will come again is a fact towards which the Christian can look with utmost confidence. *'In Him'* this prospect is as sure as though it had already taken place.

Theories relative to the details of this truth should never be allowed to divert our attention from the truth itself, nor rob us of the joy of the prospect.

IN 2 THESSALONIANS WE ARE GLORIFIED 'IN CHRIST'

Never are we allowed to forget that we are in the *world*, and in the *flesh*, and that we are surrounded by *foes*, and can meet and overcome these only super-naturally. In this Epistle Paul affirms that at last we shall be glorified in Christ (i. 12), and this means that we shall be fully and finally triumphant over every enemy—over sin, over suffering, over the flesh, over the world, over death, and over the devil.

One day we shall trample all these things beneath our feet. The Christian's goal is not death and the grave, but everlasting glory. We are not going into darkness, but into light; not into defeat, but into victory. For the Christian the best is always yet to be.

But not yet has all been said about our privileges and responsibilities 'in Christ'. So far Paul has been writing to Churches, but he has something to say to individuals also on this subject.

IN PHILEMON WE ARE MADE GRACIOUS 'IN CHRIST'

This little Note is one of the choicest things in the New Testament. Paul introduced Jesus Christ to a runaway slave in Rome, and then he sent him back to the master he had robbed, who also was a convert of the Apostle. With him he sent this Note in which he speaks of the converted slave as 'a brother beloved . . . in the Lord' (15, 16).

That statement was really the death knell of slavery, for 'in Christ' there can be 'neither bond nor free' for all are one in Him. (Gal. iii. 28).

'In Christ' the spirit of forgiveness and of forgetfulness of wrongs done takes possession of us; and in Him all wrongs are righted and all crookedness is evened out.

And now we come to the Pastoral Epistles where the words faith, faithful, and their cognates occur upwards of sixty times. This emphasis shows that 'it is required in stewards that a man be found faithful' (1 Cor. iv. 2).

And so—

IN 1 TIMOTHY WE ARE MADE FAITHFUL 'IN CHRIST'

Faithful to the doctrine the Apostles had preached; faithful to the worship, and to the oversight of the Church; faithful also in personal walk and work.

This faithfulness can be realized only '*in Christ*', but in Him it can be realized as all Christian martyrs bear witness.

We must not suppose however that Christian faithfulness is either inevitable or easy. The words *faith* and *faithful*, which occur over fifty times in the Pastoral Epistles, are rooted in the idea of *belief*, and belief implies *conviction*. Everyone should be loyal to what he believes, and if we are living consciously and joyfully '*in Christ*' we shall be true to the highest we know.

In Titus We Are Made Exemplary 'In Christ'

Writing to this young man Paul says, 'in all things shewing thyself a pattern of good works' (ii. 7). Christianity is not an ideal to be admired, but a life to be lived; it is an ethic to be preached, and also to be practised. 'Example is better than precept' is a true proverb, which '*in Christ*' we can realize.

An impressive summary of the principles of Christian conduct is given in the words:

> 'The grace of God has appeared for the salvation of all men, training us to renounce irreligion and worldly passions, and to live sober, upright, and godly lives in this world, awaiting our blessed hope the appearing of the glory of our great God and Saviour Jesus Christ' (ii. 11. 12).

In 2 Timothy We Are Triumphant 'In Christ'

In this, Paul's last Letter, is a passage of surpassing pathos and power. He has been before Nero, and is well aware that his ministry and life were drawing to a close, and in his second Letter to Timothy he pours out the fulness of his heart. How should a Christian face death?

Last words are solemn words, sometimes tragic, and sometimes glorious, as, for instance, the last words of Captain Scott, and of Nurse Cavell.

As Paul faces death he says:

> 'I am already being poured out as a drink-offering, and the time of my departure is come.
>
> 'I have fought the good fight, I have finished the course, I have kept the faith; henceforth there is laid up for me the crown of righteousness which the Lord the righteous judge shall give me at that day; and not only to me, but also to all them that have loved His appearing' (iv. 6-8).

In these immortal words the Apostle contemplates the *present* with deepest interest (6); reflects upon the *past* with calmest satisfaction (7); and anticipates the *future* with sweetest assurance (8).

That is a noble way to confront death, and it can be done only '*in Christ*'.

But this great man, though conscious that the end was at hand, did not lose interest in life and the things about him. After the foregoing great utterance he asks Timothy to collect a cloak and some parchment and books which he was forced to leave behind when suddenly rearrested at Troas, and he sends salutations to some of his friends. Truly the man who was in Rome was also '*in Christ*', and was soon to be with Him.

One more Epistle must be noticed here. Though it is not known who wrote to the Hebrews, we place this Writing, for convenience, with Paul's Letters; and we see that—

In Hebrews We Are Enriched 'In Christ'

The word '*better*' occurs more often in this Epistle than in all the rest of the New Testament. It tells of better things, a better hope, a better covenant, better promises, better sacrifice, a better possession, a better country, and a better resurrection. '*In Christ*' everything is better. This is the great fact that every Christian can test and find true—that '*in Christ*', and in Him alone, is fulness of life, of love, and of liberty; that out of Him no one truly lives, and loves, and is free. Christ is the Alpha and Omega of all good, and it is all ours in Him.

Here, then, is wealth untold. By the Blood of Atonement Christ is saving; by the Spirit of Life He is separating; and by the Word of Truth He is sanctifying.

By these means He calls, and constitutes, and characterizes His Church. 'In Him' dwelleth all the fulness of the Godhead bodily, and 'In Him we are complete'.

This is the quintessence of Christianity, and it should move us to adoring wonder and devoted living.

The messages of these Epistles are summed up in the word of the Master Himself:

'Abide in Me, and I in you. As the branch cannot bear fruit of itself, except it abide in the vine, so neither can ye, except ye abide in Me' (John xv. 4).

The truth that the Christian is '*in Christ*' is, perhaps, the greatest revelation of the New Testament, because it presupposes and includes every other truth. Were it believed and acted upon Christians would display and the world would behold what Christianity really is.

This truth includes all God's purpose for us, and excludes everything else. That we are *'in Christ'* should be the determining factor in our life, and it would be, if it were believed and trusted. It would determine our creed, our actions, our choices, our relations to others, and our whole character. But for this truth we would never have heard of the martyrs, for there would have been none.

This is the truth that has inspired the missionary enterprise; that explains why John Paton went to Tanna; why Hudson Taylor went to China; why Mary Slessor went to Calabar; why David Livingstone went to Africa; why William Carey went to India, and why innumerable men and women have sacrificed earthly comforts and temporal prospects that they might do what they believed to be the will of God for them.

This truth excludes bitterness, jealousy, ill-will, and lovelessness. It should shame us out of sectarian strife, out of petty rivalries and false ambitions, and should beget in us concord, harmony and humility.

> In Christ is love abounding,
> In Him redeeming grace;
> In Him my daily manna,
> In Him my hiding-place;
> In Him there is atonement,
> In Him eternal life;
> In Him a full salvation
> In Him an end of strife.

CHALLENGING VOICES, AND THE GOAL OF HISTORY

THE GENERAL EPISTLES AND THE REVELATION

IN tracing *How Christianity Began*, we have considered in the *Gospels, the Founder and the Foundations* of it; in the *Acts, the Greatest Adventure of All Time*, in *Paul's Epistles, a Famous Missionary's Correspondence;* and now we must look at what remains of the New Testament, the *Catholic Epistles*, which are *Challenging Voices*, and the *Book of the Revelation*, which discloses *the Goal of History*.

Aspects of Christianity

In addition to Paul's Epistles and 'Hebrews' there are seven other letters in the New Testament which are commonly called the Catholic or General Epistles —*James*, 1-2 *Peter*, 1-3 *John*, and *Jude*. There are, therefore, twenty-one Epistles in all, from the hand of six writers, and these represent different aspects of Christianity.

We may say that *Paul* represents *Gentile Christianity; James and Jude, Judaic Christianity; Peter, Mediating Christianity;* and *John, Mystical Christianity*.

They all represent Christianity but from different standpoints. The gem of Epistolary Truth has four facets. Each facet is a surface, but the gem is one; and as it is handled, now one and now another of its beauties will flash out.

We associate *Faith* with Paul; *Hope*, with Peter; *Works*, with James; *Zeal*, with Jude; and *Love*, with

John. What Paul began, Peter, James and Jude continued, and John finished.

Paul is *theological*, Peter is *experimental*, James is *ethical*, and John is *mystical*.

No one of these writers did or could present Christianity in its manifold strength and beauty, but all of them together do so. And it is still true, though Holy Scripture is no longer being written, that Christianity needs many minds and forms of presentation for the proper understanding of it. Because this is so, it is worse than foolish to compare and criticise promulgators of the truth because they do not all speak in the same terms, or adopt the same methods.

THE CATHOLIC EPISTLES

The seven Epistles we are to consider are called *Catholic* or *General*, because, unlike most of Paul's Epistles, they are not addressed to specific Churches, but to widely scattered believers.

James is 'To the Twelve Tribes which are of the Dispersion.'

1 Peter is 'To the elect who are sojourners of the Dispersion in Pontus, Galatia, Cappadocia, Asia, and Bithynia'.

2 Peter is 'To them that have obtained a like precious faith with us in the righteousness of our God and Saviour Jesus Christ'.

1 John has no introduction.

2 John is 'Unto the elect lady and her children'.

3 John is 'Unto Gaius the beloved'; and

Jude is 'To them that are called, beloved in God the Father, and kept for Jesus Christ'.

Each of these seven Epistles has a distinct and

challenging message for Christians to-day, as they had for those who first read them, and it is to these messages that attention is now invited.

We have seen that in each of Paul's Epistles the life of the believer, a life lived 'in Christ', is presented in some definite aspect. In Him we are justified, and sanctified, and liberated, and so on; and this 'in Christ' life is further revealed in the Catholic Epistles.

We see in the Epistle of *James* that 'in Christ' we are made *consistent;* by becoming, not hearers only of the Word, but doers of it also (i. 22-25). In *1 Peter* we are shown how to become *true disciples* by following Him who has left us an example (ii. 21-23). In *2 Peter* only 'in Christ' can we attain to the *knowledge* whereby we can 'grow in grace' (iii. 18). In *1 John* we learn the secret of *abiding* 'in Christ', who is the divine Light, and Love, and Life (ii. 28). In *2 John* we are told that they who are 'in Christ' should be *loyal* to His person, Who is God manifest in the flesh (7-10). In *3 John* we are shown how we may *fulfil* our Christian opportunities 'in Christ' and how we may *default*. In *Jude's Epistle* we learn that because Christ in His love *keeps* us, we should *keep* ourselves in His love (i. 21).

We have, then, in the Epistles, twenty-one aspects of blessings which are the Christian's 'in Christ', and in these areas of truth we may well say of ourselves, 'there remaineth yet very much land to be possessed' (Josh xiii. 1).

Let us now turn first of all to—

THE MESSAGE OF JAMES

At the outset it is more than interesting to note that

one of Jesus' brothers is the writer of this Epistle, because before the crucifixion His brethren did not
believe in Him (John vii. 5); that is, they did not know
who He was, and did not credit His Messianic claims.
But in resurrection life Jesus appeared to James (1 Cor.
xv. 7), and after that he was, as he says, 'a bondslave
of God and of the Lord Jesus Christ' (i. 1).

This Writing is called an Epistle, but there is nothing
epistolary about it. The address is impersonal, and
there are no salutations; and on examination it will be
seen that the writer deals with a number of subjects,
which are not necessarily related to one another. They
may be summaries of sermons which James had
preached in Jerusalem.

These subjects are of an intensely practical character,
and show that James is *the Apostle of applied Christianity*.

He says that hearing the Word of God is of no use
unless we do it (i. 19-27): that paying respect to persons
because of their social position, or their possession of
money, is anti-Christian (ii. 1-13): that a claim to
faith is of no value unless and until it is demonstrated
by works (ii. 14-26): that if we do not control our
tongues we are like horses without bits, like ships
without rudders, like untamed beasts, and like a
match that sets a forest on fire.

Gossip, and lying, and duplicity, bear no relation
to Christianity, and of these no Christian should be
guilty.

James speaks also of false wisdom, of censoriousness,
and of profanity. His idea of Christianity does not
consist in hymn-singing and meeting-attending, but
in carrying out in detail, everywhere, and all the time,
the faith we profess.

Secondly:

THE MESSAGE OF PETER

This Apostle wrote two Epistles, and each has its distinctive message.

The design of the *First Epistle* was to comfort and strengthen his fellow-believers in the sufferings to which they were exposed, and to assure them of final triumph; and this is his message to us also. The Epistle is full of consolation, and it assures the believer that, in spite of inevitable sufferings, the horizon is bright.

It is pre-eminently the *Epistle of Hope*. There is here no make-believe about the Christian life; the facts, however, should not depress, but rather should stimulate to a greater reliance on, and enjoyment of Christ who is our Example; Who, 'when He was reviled, reviled not again; and when He suffered, threatened not, but committed His cause to Him that judgeth righteously' (ii. 23).

Summarily the Apostle has three things to say to us: first, that the *Vocation of the Christian is Salvation* (i. 3-ii.10); secondly, that *the Behaviour of the Christian should be characterized by Submission* (ii. 11-iii. 12); and thirdly, that *the Discipline of the Christian is by Suffering* (iii. 13-v. 11).

The ideas of *Salvation*, *Submission*, and *Suffering* constitute Peter's message.

Salvation was the theme of the past; it is the joy of the present; and also it is the hope of the future. In Peter's presentation salvation is much more than regeneration; it embraces the whole of Christian experience until this is consummated in glory.

Submission, as here taught, is not weakness, but strength; submission civil, social, and conjugal. It represents an attitude to life which is based on principle and not on the Christian's changing moods and circumstances.

Suffering in this Epistle is not penal, but disciplinary, and the spheres of it are the World (iii. 13-iv. 6), the Church (iv. 7-v. 7), and the Heavenlies (v. 8-11).

The design of the *Second Epistle* is *to remind us of the things we already know.* Peter says:

> 'I will not be negligent to put you always in remembrance of these things, though ye know them'.
> 'I think it meet to stir you up by putting you in remembrance'.
> 'This is now the second Epistle that I write unto you; and in both of them I stir up your sincere mind by putting you in remembrance' (i. 12, 13; iii. 1. 2).

The message then of this Epistle is *remember what you know,* and this goes well with the message of James, *do what you profess.*

In 2 Peter *the knowledge of God* is related to the Christian's *Growth* (i. 2-21); to his *Peril* (ii. 1-22); and to his *Hope* (iii. 1-18).

Relative to the *growth,* a famous passage is chapter i. 5-11, where its progress is traced from *faith,* through *virtue, knowledge, self-control, patience,* and *godliness,* to *love.*

When the Christian thus grows he will be preserved from the ever-present peril of false teaching (ii) and will continuously rejoice in the prospect of Christ's Return (iii).

Jesus said to the regenerated Peter, 'when you are converted strengthen your brethren' (Luke xxii, 32), and truly this he has done. The man who denied his Lord three times has written two Epistles of superlative importance to all Christians. He is an outstanding proof of the fact that none of us needs to be paralysed by the past, and also of the truth that even our failures can be turned to account for the safeguarding of our brethren, and so be made to promote the glory of God.

Thirdly:

THE MESSAGE OF JUDE

That the Christian is ever in peril Jude affirms. He had intended to write about 'salvation', but news reached him which changed his purpose and constrained him to write a letter of warning, and of denunciation of evil persons who privily had crept into the Church (4).

In the light of this peril the Christian has a threefold duty. The first is *Biblical;* we must study the Scriptures (17-19); the second is *Personal*; we must 'keep ourselves' in the love of God by 'building up ourselves on our most holy faith; and praying in the Holy Spirit' (20, 21); and the third is *Relative;* we have a duty to them who are in doubt, to them who are in danger, and to them who have departed from the faith (22. 23).

This short Epistle is of great importance, and its benediction is second to none.

'Now unto Him who is able to guard you from stumbling, and to set you before the presence of His glory without blemish in exceeding joy, to the only God our Saviour, through Jesus Christ our Lord, be glory, majesty, dominion and power, before all time, and now, and for evermore. Amen' (24, 25).

Fourthly:

THE MESSAGE OF JOHN

The Apostle John has contributed to the New Testament five Writings—a *Gospel, Three Epistles,* and an *Apocalypse.*

In the *Gospel* he shows that the Man of Galilee was God; in the *Epistles* he shows that it was God who became Man; and in the *Apocalypse* he shows that ultimate victory over all evil will be by and for the God-Man.

In the *Gospel* Christ is in the *world;* in the *Epistles* He is in the *heart;* and in the *Apocalypse* He is in the *Church.*

The Johannine Writings are the last in the New Testament, and are, in a very real sense, a summary of the whole.

JOHN'S FIRST EPISTLE

The Apostle states clearly what his object was in writing. It was that we Christians may have fellowship with one another; that our joy may be full; that we may not sin; that we may know, upon confession, that our sins are forgiven; and that we may have full assurance of eternal life.

The Epistle is not like any other Writing in the New Testament, but is in a category by itself. In it profoundest thought is presented in simplest language;

its style is rhythmical and antithetical; and it is characterized by calm serenity, by a tone of authority, and by a sense of finality.

All its subjects are great, and are treated greatly; *Christ, sin, the world, antichrist, hate, love, error, truth, righteousness, belief,* and *eternal life.*

Broadly speaking—for the Epistle does not lend itself easily to analysis—we may say that here three subjects are treated:

> the Christian's *Advance in the Light Divine;*
> the Christian's *Attitude towards the Love Divine;* and
> the Christian's *Affinity with the Life Divine.*

The subjects of *sin and sinning* are handled by this Apostle with a firmness scarcely found elsewhere.

He says:

> 'If we say that we have no sin, we deceive ourselves'. (i. 8.)
> 'If we say that we have not sinned, we make God a liar'. (i. 10.)
> 'If any man sin, we have an Advocate with the Father'. (ii. 1.)
> 'Whosoever abideth in Christ sinneth not'. (iii.6.)
> The Christian 'cannot sin because he is begotten of God'. (iii. 9.)
> 'Whosoever is begotten of God doeth no sin'. (iii.9.)

These statements are not contradictory, nor are they expressions of wishful thinking; but they clearly distinguish between *the committal of single acts of sin,* and *continuing in a course of sin.*

The Epistle does not teach that sin is *extracted* from our nature; neither does it teach that we must keep *suppressing* it, and with little effect; but it does teach, as does Paul, that the law of the Spirit of life in Christ Jesus makes us free from the law of sin and of death (Rom. viii. 2). This is the great truth of *counteraction*, of one law negativing another.

'*Sin is lawlessness*', John says; and when we sin we break the law in three directions—*Godward, selfward,* and *manward*.

John's teaching on Truth and Error circles round the Person of Christ. Rival spirits must be tested, and the test is their attitude to Him. Every heresy in the world is an attack, in some way, upon the Person and Work of Christ.

Evolution makes Christ the mere product of a sinful race. Theosophy places Him on a level with Confucius, Plato, and Buddha as a great teacher.

Christian Science declares that Christ was not God, but only a divine ideal.

Spiritualism affirms that Christ is nothing more than a medium of high order.

Russellism denies the Deity of Christ, and His resurrection.

Rationalistic Criticism rejects the infallibility of Christ, and sits in judgment on His pronouncements.

Modernism denies the Virgin Birth, the Deity, and the Atonement of Christ.

Nazism puts the State in the place of Christ.

Communism dethrones Christ by enthroning Karl Marx.

'Jesus Christ is the storm-centre; the battle sways this way and that about the person of the King. Every kind of antipathy that Christianity excites, in the modern, as in the ancient world, impinges on our Lord's name and person; its shafts strike on the great shield of the Captain of salvation, from whatever quarter they are aimed'.

The importance of this First Epistle of John cannot be exaggerated.

John's Second Epistle

The value of this Letter of only 244 words is not to be determined by its length. It strikes two great notes, and strikes them firmly—the notes of Love and Truth. Love is the energy of the Christian life, and Truth is the principle of it.

The conjunction of these ideas is impressive. To walk only in Truth would make one hard; and to walk only in Love would make one soft, but to walk in them both makes one strong.

The Apostle points out that Christians are in danger of departing from the Truth in respect of the Person of Christ who is the crucial test of all doctrine (7-11).

The foundation of Christian fellowship is laid in the Divine-human Person of Christ and His atoning sacrifice, and if these are denied there is nothing left on which to build.

To-day there is much talk about reunion and ecumenicity, and many Christians are in doubt about their relation to all this, and wonder if there is any sure guidance.

Well, there is. Paul and John make it abundantly clear that there can be no Christian fellowship where the New Testament doctrine of the Person and Work of Christ is denied or compromised. 'What communion hath light with darkness, or what part hath he that believeth with an infidel?' He who denies the true divinity, the sinless humanity, and the atoning sacrifice of Christ is an infidel, whatever his ecclesiastical profession and standing may be, and a true Christian can have no fellowship with such.

There are people who claim to be *advanced* thinkers in matters related to the Christian religion, and who regard with more or less of pity those who are not. Touching one matter the Apostle John has something to say about such people, and this is it:

> 'Every one *leading-forward* and not abiding in
> the doctrine which is Christ's hath not God' (9).

This word '*leading-forward*' includes two ideas: first, *going beyond* the line of truth in what seems to be an *advance;* and secondly, *leading* others in this so-called advanced direction.

With these *advanced* thinkers we are to have no fellowship. There is such a thing as heresy, and to tolerate it is sinful compromise. There are times when intolerance is simply loyalty to Christ. We must, however, be very careful not to regard as a heretic everyone who differs from ourselves in any and every matter. Orthodoxy and heresy are determined by one's doctrine of Christ. The supreme question is, 'What think ye of Christ?'

JOHN'S THIRD EPISTLE

Here three men are brought to our notice—Gaius, Diotrephes, and Demetrius. *Gaius* is a well-to-do layman, noted for his hospitality. *Diotrephes* is a Church official, noted for his haughtiness and arrogance, and *Demetrius* is an evangelist, noted for his humility and faithfulness.

These are persons of the first century, and of the

twentieth also. Perhaps some of you have all three in your Church. Well, read what John has to say about them; especially about the person who loves to have the pre-eminence, and call the attention of your Diotrephes to this latest photo of himself. But do not forget to thank Gaius, and to encourage Demetrius.

These two epistolary Notes should be carefully studied. It is impressive that in the canon of Holy Scripture should be included these two brief private letters, one to a woman, and one to a man; but together they condemn two evils to which Christians and the Christian Church are ever exposed, the evils of *heresy* and *schism*. The 'deceivers' represent the one, and Diotrephes, the other.

But side by side with these condemnations are generous commendations—of Kyria, and Gaius, and Demetrius.

Condemnation only is unjust, and commendation only is unwise; and so we should pray for insight and courage.

The Goal of History

And now we come to the last book of the New Testament, the *Revelation*, in which the veil is drawn aside to show us the *goal of history*.

Not without reason did the early Church study this Book. Practically the whole of it is reproducible from the Christian writers of the first three centuries, and it is probably true that this cannot be said of any other New Testament Writing.

The interpretation of the Book has always been a subject of controversy, but it has values which rise above all controversy, and which make it a Book of superlative importance. It is with these values that we are now concerned.

Whether or not this was the last Book of the New Testament to be written we cannot say, but in being put last it certainly is in its right place, for it takes us to the goal of history, and beyond that we cannot go.

As no other Book, the Revelation stands in certain relations to all other parts of the Bible, a fact which gives the seal of finality to it. Take two illustrations only. First,

ITS RELATION TO THE WHOLE BIBLE

In *Genesis* is the *Foundation* of God's redeeming purpose, in *Exodus to Jude,* the *Superstructure* of it, and in *Revelation,* the *Completion* of it.

Genesis is the *Beginning, Exodus to Jude* is the *Way,* and *Revelation* is the *End.*

In *Genesis* are *Origins,* in *Exodus to Jude* are *Processes,* and in *Revelation* are *Issues.*

The *Old Testament* is about the *Kingdom;* the *Gospels* are about the *Messiah;* the *Epistles* are about *the Church;* and *the Revelation is about them all.*

The second illustration is

ITS RELATION TO THE BOOK OF GENESIS

The first and last Books of the Bible present most striking comparisons and contrasts.

By way of comparison:

In *Genesis* are the *First Heaven and Earth,* and in *Revelation,* the *Last.* In *Genesis* is the *First Rest,* and in *Revelation,* the *Final Rest.* In *Genesis Paradise is Lost,* and in *Revelation* it is *Regained*. In *Genesis* are *Trees and Rivers,* and in *Revelation* the *Tree and the River*. In *Genesis* are *Husband and Wife,* and in *Revelation,* the *Lamb and the Bride*.

But the contrasts between these two Books are even more striking.

In the first, *Satan is victorious;* in the last, he is *defeated*. In the first, *judgment is pronounced;* and in the last it is *executed*. In the first, the *Divine face is hidden;* and in the last, *we see His face*. In the first, *the gates are shut against us;* and in the last, *they are never shut*. In the first, Adam and Eve were *banished from the Tree of Life;* and in the last, *we have a right to it*. In the first, we were *exiles from the earthly garden;* and in the last, we are *inheritors of the heavenly city*.

Whatever interpretation of this Book one follows—Praeterist, Historicist, Futurist, or Idealist—it has values which all interpreters must acknowledge.

We mention two only of these.

First of all, this Book is,

An Unveiling of the Lord Jesus Christ

Its opening sentence declares this, and the whole Book proves it. In three distinct ways is He revealed—in His *nature,* in His *activities,* and in His *manifold relations*.

As to His Nature: this is revealed in His names and titles. He is the Lord, the Word, Jesus, Christ, Master, King, Lamb, Lion, Morning Star, Alpha and Omega, Beginning and End, First and Last.

As to His Activities: He is revealed as Chastening the Church, Restoring Israel, and Judging the World.

As to His Relations: these are to heaven, and earth, and hell. To the Father, the Holy Spirit, and unfallen angels; to saints and sinners; and to fallen angels and doomed people. Only the Gospels reveal Christ more fully than does this last Book of the Bible; but whereas there He is seen in humiliation, here He is seen in glory.

Of all aspects of the revelation of Christ in this Book none is more wonderful than the presentation of Him as the LAMB. There are two words in the New Testament for 'lamb', but the one used throughout this Book means 'the little Lamb', and it occurs 28 times.

The idea of the Lamb in the Bible is related to sacrifice and redemption; and this last Book shows us that the Lamb that was slain on Calvary is now on 'the Throne of God' (xxii. 1, 3). The Cross triumphs at last.

In the second place this Book is:

A REVELATION OF THE ISSUE OF HISTORY

It is full of sharp contrasts of persons and forces in conflict with one another: Christ and Antichrist; the Church and the World; Living Creatures and Beasts; Angels unfallen and fallen; the Deity and the Dragon; Jerusalem and Babylon; Righteousness and Iniquity; Truth and Error; Light and Darkness; Holiness and Sin; Paradise and the Pit.

Such contrasts and conflicts have characterized all the ages, and are particularly pronounced at the present time; and people of all nations are wistfully asking—'what will the end be?'

This Book answers that question. It tells us that Christ, not Antichrist will triumph; the Church, not the World; the Deity, not the Dragon; Truth, not Error; Right, not Wrong; Light, not Darkness.

The day is assuredly coming when 'the Kingdom of this world will become the Kingdom of our Lord and of His Christ, and He shall reign for ever and ever'.

A great Voice in heaven will say:

> 'Now is come the salvation, and the power, and the kingdom of our God, and the authority of His Christ; for the accuser of our brethren is cast down, which accused them before our God day and night. And they overcame him because of the blood of the Lamb'. (xii. 10-11.)
>
> 'And God shall wipe away every tear; and death shall be no more; neither shall there be mourning, nor crying, nor pain any more. He that sitteth on the Throne will make all things new.' (xxi. 4-5.)

The last thing will not be the intellect of Athens, nor the luxury of Babylon, nor the power of Rome, nor the fashion of Paris, nor the commerce of New York, nor the splendour of London, but the New Jerusalem, which stands for religion and character, which shall descend out of heaven from God.

The last thing will *not be bombs, but blessings; not war, but peace; not uncertainty but confidence; not sickness, but health; not weakness, but strength; not longing, but satisfaction; not sorrow, but joy; not weariness, but vigour.*

There's a great time coming, so let us lift up our heads and our hearts, for the day of our redemption draweth nigh.

Printed at the Press of the Publishers